Inspired to Learn. empowered for life.

Valley Montessori School
1273 North Livermore Ave.
Livemore, CA 94551

★ IT'S MY STATE! ★
Minnesota

Marlene Targ Brill

BENCHMARK BOOKS

MARSHALL CAVENDISH
NEW YORK

Series Consultant

David G. Vanderstel, Ph.D., Executive Director, National Council on Public History

Benchmark Books
Marshall Cavendish
99 White Plains Road
Tarrytown, New York 10591-9001
www.marshallcavendish.com

Text, maps, and illustrations © 2004 by Marshall Cavendish Corporation
Maps and illustrations by Christopher Santoro

Library of Congress Cataloging-in-Publication Data

Brill, Marlene Targ.
Minnesota / by Marlene Targ Brill.
p. cm. — (It's my state!)
Summary: Surveys the history, geography, government, and economy of
Minnesota as well as the diverse ways of life of its people.
Includes bibliographical references (p.) and index.
ISBN 0-7614-1534-3
1. Minnesota—Juvenile literature. [1. Minnesota.]
I. Title. II.Series.

F606.3.B75 2003
977.6—dc21
2002156734

Photo research by Candlepants, Inc.

Cover photo: Layne Kennedy / Corbis
Back cover illustration: The license plate shows Minnesota's postal abbreviation, followed by its year of statehood.

The photographs in this book are used by permission and through the courtesy of: *Corbis:* 35, 50 (top); Bettmann, 41 (top), 51 (top); Layne Kennedy, 4 (bottom), 70 (middle); Tom Bean, 10; Dave G. Houser, 11; Joseph Sohm, 12; W. Perry Conway, 16; Anne Laird, 17 (top); Richard Hamilton Smith, 18 (bottom), 58, 67, 68, 71 (bottom); Phil Schermeister, 49; AFP, 50 (middle); Douglas Kirkland, 50 (bottom); Jay Dickman, 51 (bottom); Raymond Gehman, 54; Richard Cummins, 56; Marlen Raabe, 66; Ed Kashi, 71 (middle). *Animals Animals / Earth Scenes:* Don Enger, 4 (top), 20; Erwin & Peggy Bauer, 17 (bottom); Azure Computer & Photo Services, 18 (top). *Getty Images:* Tom Walker / The Image Bank, 19 (bottom). *Minnesota Historical Society:* 38; Photo by John Krueth, 22; Artist: Seth Eastman, 24; Artist: Dewey Albinson, 28; Artist: John Casper Wild, 30; Artist: Ferdinand Reichardt, 31; Artist: J.C. Dollman, 34; Photo by Harry D. Ayer, 37; Photo by Lee Brothers, 39; Photo by Kathy Drozen, 41 (bottom). *Index Stock Imagery:* Lawrence Sawyer, 8; Amy Wiley/Wales, 13; Kent Dufault, 44; Blue Water Photo, 55; CLEO Freelance, 61; Michael Siluk, 63. *The Image Works:* Frozen Images, 4 (middle); Skjold, 42, 47, 53; Mike Siluk, 48, 52; David Fraizer, 71 (top). *Envision:* Steven Needham, 5 (top), 70 (bottom); Madeline Polss, 5 (bottom); MAK Studio, 19 (top); Mark Ferri, 19 (middle); Peter Johansky, 70 (top). *Bill Lindner Photography:* 18 (middle). *Art Resource, NY:* Smithsonian American Art Museum, Washington, DC, 25. *Moose Lake State Park:* 5 (middle). *C.E. Mitchell/Blackstar:* 51 (middle). *Paul Stafford :* 15, 45, 46, 64, 72, 74.

Series design by Anahid Hamparian

Printed in Italy

1 3 5 6 4 2

Contents

A Quick Look at Minnesota

Nickname: North Star State, Gopher State, and
the Land of 10,000 Lakes

Population: 4,919,479 (2000)

Statehood: 1858

Tree: Norway Pine

*Most of the Norway pines in Minnesota are
found in the northern and northeastern parts
of the state. As the tree ages, the bark begins to
turn a reddish color, which is why this tree is
also known as the red pine.*

Bird: Common Loon

*This black-feathered, red-eyed bird can be seen
gliding gently across the waters in northern,
northeastern, and central Minnesota. Loons can
dive into the water in search of food and may
stay underwater for nearly five
minutes. They can also fly at
speeds of up to 60 miles per hour.
However, they look clumsy
when they walk on land.*

Flower: Pink and White Lady Slipper

*Lady slippers dot Minnesota's canoe country with their
pink and white bowl-like flowers. The plants grow slowly,
taking four to sixteen years to flower. Some of these plants
can live up to fifty years and may grow 4 feet high.*

4

State Muffin: Blueberry

Third-grade children chose the blueberry muffin as the state muffin in 1988. They felt that the main ingredients in the muffins—blueberries and wheat—were important to the state. Wild blueberries grow in the swamps, forests, and hills of northeastern Minnesota. Farmers all around the state grow wheat.

State Gemstone: Lake Superior Agate

Lake Superior Agate was formed millions of years ago by geological forces such as flowing lava and moving glaciers. Red and orange bands line these special quartz stones. The agate's reddish color comes from the iron found in the ground. Sometimes the rocks are polished and used in jewelry such as rings or necklaces.

State Drink: Milk

Minnesota cows produce almost nine billion pounds of milk each year. That amount ranks fifth in the nation. This is one of the reasons why Minnesotans chose milk as the state drink in 1984.

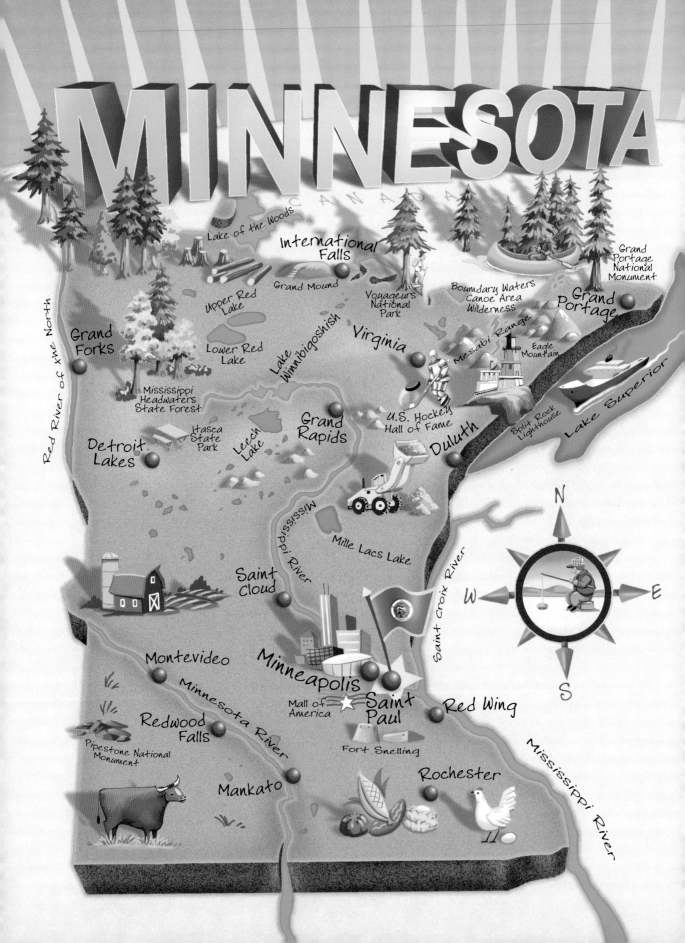

MINNESOTA

CANADA

Lake of the Woods

International Falls

Grand Mound

Upper Red Lake

Lower Red Lake

Voyageurs National Park

Boundary Waters Canoe Area Wilderness

Grand Portage National Monument

Grand Portage

Virginia

Mesabi Range

Eagle Mountain

Red River of the North

Grand Forks

Lake Winnibigoshish

Mississippi Headwaters State Forest

U.S. Hockey Hall of Fame

Split Rock Lighthouse

Lake Superior

Itasca State Park

Leech Lake

Grand Rapids

Detroit Lakes

Duluth

Mississippi River

Mille Lacs Lake

Saint Croix River

Saint Cloud

N

W   E

S

Montevideo

Minneapolis

Minnesota River

Mall of America

Saint Paul

Red Wing

Redwood Falls

Pipestone National Monument

Fort Snelling

Mississippi River

Mankato

Rochester

The Land of 10,000 Lakes

Minnesota contains many sky-blue waters, blankets of forest, and acres of sweeping fertile flatland. These different land-forms, plus a wide range of weather from north to south, make Minnesota seem like several states in one.

Minnesotans have always loved their still, blue waters. The name Minnesota comes from the Dakota word *minisota*, which means "water that reflects the sky." Sparkling waterways are one of the state's most striking features. Many proud Minnesotans have license plates that read "Land of 10,000 Lakes." But Minnesota really has more than 15,000 lakes. Three-quarters of these lakes are at least 10 acres in area.

Together the state's rivers and lakes offer more shoreline than Hawaii, Florida, and California combined. Water flows out of Minnesota in three directions. It flows north into Canada's Hudson Bay, south toward the Gulf of Mexico, and east toward the Atlantic Ocean.

Minnesota's Borders
North: Canada
South: Iowa
East: Wisconsin
West: North Dakota and South Dakota

Minnesota's many lakes, rivers, and land features were formed over thousands of years of geological change.

There is no doubt that Minnesota is lake country. But where did they all come from? Scientists say the lakes developed over many years. About ten thousand years ago, most of Minnesota was covered by glaciers—huge sheets of slow-moving ice. Some glaciers were more than a mile thick. As they crept along, the glaciers sliced off mountaintops and dug out valleys. As the glaciers moved, they also deposited soil, sand, and rocks. When the last glacier disappeared, the face of the land had been greatly changed. Soil filled with brush and rocks covered the future state. Melting ice filled in deep holes to form lakes and rivers.

Today, the state is known for the features some of the glaciers helped create. Minnesota has rugged cliffs, rolling hills, and flat prairies. The state can be divided into different regions. Each of Minnesota's main regions is home to its own unique landforms that feature different climates, plants, and animals.

> *. . . now letters and newspapers . . . had begun to tell . . . of a beautiful country with lakes and rivers thick with fish, forests full of game, and fertile acres on which farms would flourish.*
> —Helen Clapesattle in *The Doctors Mayo*

Grassland Plains and Prairies

At one time, a large inland sea called Lake Agassiz covered western Minnesota. The lake covered an area larger than all of the Great Lakes combined. When the lake dried, it left a stretch of flat land that contained some of the most fertile soil in the world. The region is called the Red River Valley. The area is known for its oats, corn, and bright yellow sunflowers.

The rolling green hills of Minnesota's prairies cover some of the state's most fertile soil.

Prairies mix with sweeping farm fields in the southwest. Once Dakota Indians herded buffalo across the grassy plains. As settlers arrived, they cleared the prairie cactus and colorful wildflowers to create farmland. Pockets of woods interrupt the gentle views of the plains. These woods shelter wildlife during Minnesota's cold winters and hot summers.

Headwaters

A network of lakes, rivers, and swamps form much of north-central Minnesota. Corn and soybean fields in the south give way to thick forests of pine and leafy trees in the north. This is the Headwaters region, famous for Lake Itasca, which lies in Minnesota's oldest state park, Itasca State Park.

Children wade in the shallow waters of the Mississippi River's headwaters at Itasca State Park.

Why is such a small lake so important? Its name, which comes from parts of the Latin words veritas for "truth" and caput for "head," gives you a clue. Lake Itasca is the beginning, or "true head," of the Mississippi River. From there, the mighty river travels south about 2,340 miles to the Gulf of Mexico. Starting as a trickle, the waters of the Mississippi grow into the largest waterway in North America and the third largest in the world.

This region contains one of the crown jewels of Minnesota lakes. Lake of the Woods is the largest freshwater lake in the country after the five Great Lakes. More than 14,000 islands pepper the water. The lake includes more than 2,000 square miles of sandy beaches, marshy shoreline, and loads of walleye fish.

Arrowhead

Northeastern Minnesota is shaped like an arrowhead, with Canada to the north and Lake Superior to the east. The region includes thick woods, clear lakes, and fast-flowing rapids. There you will see Eagle Mountain, the tallest peak in the state, stretching up 2,301 feet. Lake Superior makes up 150 miles of the area's varied shoreline. From the often icy water, boaters can see cliffs soaring 1,000 feet tall, waterfalls, and forests of maple, pine, and birch trees. Besides offering amazing beauty, Lake Superior serves as an inland port. By using the lake's connection to the other Great Lakes, Minnesota is connected to the eastern part of the country.

The Arrowhead region is famous for its Boundary Waters

Split Rock Lighthouse sits on a cliff overlooking Lake Superior's north shore.

Canoe Area Wilderness. Here more than 1,000 lakes and streams cut through lush forests. Boaters can travel for hours, stopping to fish or enjoy the area's peaceful beauty.

Nearby is the Mesabi Range, where rocky cliffs zigzag 120 miles from Hoyt Lakes to Grand Rapids. In 1890, a miner discovered iron in the range. From then on, the miners who came to the region called it Mountain Iron. The Mesabi Range gets its name from an Ojibwe legend about a red giant named Mesabe who slept in the earth.

Bluffland

Glaciers never reached the southeastern corner of Minnesota. That is why this area looks different from the rest of the state. Rolling farmland covers parts of the landscape. Farther east, limestone bluffs rise like towers above the Mississippi River.

Minnesota's waterways offer many opportunities to observe the state's natural beauty.

Cave-filled hills line rivers that have carved paths through rock. The area is another part of Minnesota known for its wonderful views.

The Climate

Minnesotans joke that their state's climate is "ten months of winter and two months of rough sledding." Snow covers much of the state from mid-December to mid-March. Sudden blizzards, gusty winds, and snow drifts are a constant threat. There is no question about it, Minnesota gets very cold.

I love the outdoor fun Minnesota has to offer. Minnesota is my favorite vacation spot.
—A visitor to the state

During the 1800s, Minnesotans liked to brag about the state's freezing temperatures. One writer claimed, "It [the climate] was without an equal in healthfulness. Its cold, clear air made the lungs . . . whole again, brought color to . . . cheeks and vigor [energy] to weakened bodies."

Today not everyone agrees. Many people find adjusting to such extreme cold difficult. Frostbite and the risk of freezing keep Minnesotans bundled up for much of the year. Below-zero temperatures vary by about 15 degrees from north to south. Temperatures dip below freezing more than thirty-four days a year in the south and sixty-eight days in the north. International Falls in northern Minnesota reported the state's coldest recorded temperature in 1996—a frosty minus 60 degrees Fahrenheit.

In some big cities, many workers and shoppers travel between downtown buildings through enclosed paths called skyways. At night, some Minnesotans plug their cars into

Freezing temperatures and snow do not stop Minnesotans from enjoying the outdoors.

electric warmers to keep their engines from freezing. But for those who love winter sports, Minnesota is a paradise. Frozen lakes provide the perfect places to skate, sled, snowmobile, and play ice hockey. When ice on the lakes freezes 12 inches thick, many people go ice-fishing. Some drive onto the lake, bring a small shelter to block the wind, and dig a hole in the ice to drop in their fishing line.

Minnesota weather is more than ice and snow. Spring and summer can be hot and humid. Rainfall increases throughout the state from west to east. The rain feeds the thick forests and fast-running streams. Springtime tornadoes can whip across the plains, leaving a path of destruction.

Temperatures can reach record highs in July and August. The highest temperature ever recorded in the state was 114 degrees Fahrenheit in Moorhead on July 6, 1936. Temperatures drop as you travel north. Minnesotans who prefer cooler weather head north to the shores of Lake Superior for the summer. The water in the massive lake helps to moderate extreme temperatures throughout the year. It acts like a giant air conditioner in summer and a heater in winter.

Wildlife

With its varied geography, Minnesota is home to many types of plant and animal life. One-third of the state is filled with trees. You can find balsam fir, black spruce, and white cedar growing in the northern woods. Eastern white pine trees are common throughout the northern, eastern,

A bobcat rests in a maple tree.

and central portions of Minnesota. Trees such as cottonwood, American elm, and bur oak grow across the state. In the fall, the leaves of sugar maples in eastern Minnesota turn beautiful shades of orange, red, and yellow.

Minnesota's Department of Natural Resources has its own native big tree registry. Minnesotans are encouraged to find and report very large native trees. The trees are measured, and the largest ones are declared champions.

Many types of flowers bloom in Minnesota. These include jack-in-the-pulpit, starflowers, trillium, bunchberry, and asters. Goldenrods spread across Minnesota's meadows. The state is home to more than ten different types of goldenrod. In some of the state swamps you may find pitcher plants. These insect-eating plants can grow to be almost 2 feet tall.

The fields and forests of Minnesota are also home to deer, beavers, raccoons, and squirrels. In the woods you may see skunks, porcupines, and red and gray foxes. Gray foxes are special because they are the only member of the dog family that can climb trees. Pine martens—also known as American martens—live in Minnesota's forests. They are related to weasels and were once thought to be extinct in Minnesota. However, starting in the 1980s, growing marten populations were found in the northern part of the state.

A pine marten peeks out from a hole in a tree.

Other animals in Minnesota include moose, elk, and black bears. Northern Minnesota has one of the largest black bear populations in the United States. The howls of gray wolves, timber wolves, and coyote often pierce the night.

A coyote mother and her six-week-old pup howl in the North Woods

Plants & Animals

Gray Wolf

Gray wolves often travel in packs that can have anywhere from two to fifteen members. Once nearly extinct, these wolves are now protected by law. Over two thousand wolves roam freely across pockets of the state.

Walleye

Big eyes with large white circles around them give this popular fish its name. Because of its large eyes, a walleye has excellent night vision. This fish is an important part of Minnesota's huge fishing industry. One of the largest walleyes caught in Minnesota weighed 17 pounds 8 ounces. It was pulled from Saganaga Lake, the state's deepest lake, in 1979.

Monarch Butterfly

Minnesota is home to many different types of butterflies. Unlike most butterflies, monarchs travel south for the winter. Some fly up to 80 miles a day from Minnesota to warm regions of central Mexico.

Morel Mushroom

These brown, spongy-topped mushrooms add an unusual flavor to many different foods. Each spring, expert mushroom hunters search Minnesota's fields and forests for morels. But mushroom hunters must carefully identify the morels before picking them. This is because some kinds of mushrooms are poisonous and should never be eaten.

Wild Rice

Wild rice can be found in many shallow bodies of water in northern and central Minnesota. This plant has been used throughout Minnesota's history. The Native Americans who lived in the area hundreds of years ago harvested and ate the rice. Minnesotans still grow and harvest wild rice today.

Beaver

This large rodent can be found in the waters and woods around the state. It uses its sharp teeth to cut down trees to use for building dams. A beaver's tail is flat and shaped like a paddle, which helps the animal move through the water.

Forster's terns nest in Minnesota's marshes and along its beaches, rivers, and lakes.

Minnesota has a large bird population. The state lies at the northern edge of the Mississippi flyway. The flyway is a migration route for millions of birds. Canada geese, hawks, mallard and wood ducks, and gadwalls spend summers in Minnesota. Loons, grouse, pheasants, and wild turkey also thrive in Minnesota. Other types of birds, such as bald eagles and falcons, can be seen flying through the region. Their populations were threatened by harmful chemicals such as DDT, which was used to kill insects. Now many harmful substances have been banned. Without deadly poisons to kill or harm them, the birds have slowly grown in number.

Different aquatic, or water-loving, animals thrive in Minnesota. Several types of salamander, frogs, snakes, and turtles live in and around the state's waterways. Minnesota's waters are home to almost 153 species, or types, of fish. Most of them are native to the state. These fish have helped to create the state's large and profitable fishing industry. Each year countless numbers of residents and visitors fish for bass, trout, walleye, and northern pike. President Theodore Roosevelt's uncle, Robert Roosevelt, wrote that in Minnesota "every river swarms, every bay is a reservoir [store] of magnificent fish."

Preservation and Protection

State and local governments work together with residents to preserve and protect Minnesota's resources and wildlife. Laws have been passed to prevent people from disturbing the habitats of animals that are threatened. In Minnesota, as in other states, it is also illegal to interfere with endangered animals with very small populations. To protect the healthy populations of other animals, the government puts limits on hunting and trapping. For example, in order to protect the number of walleye around Mille Lacs, lawmakers control the number of fishers allowed into the region.

Minnesotans are also concerned about protecting their forests. The logging industry is important to the state economy, but Betsy Daub, Minnesota Audubon forest director, says that "[86] percent of the Superior National Forest and 73 percent of the Ojibwe land are managed for one goal—timber." Daub hopes that the state can create a plan that puts plants and animals before logging and recreation.

In 1981, the state created the Minnesota Conservation Corps (MCC) so that citizens could become involved in saving natural resources. Through this agency, students work with professionals to help preserve and restore the environment. Group projects include building trails and log shelters, improving the forest or park campgrounds, and exploring ways to stop forest fires and to reduce harm to fish.

2 From the Beginning

Thousands of years ago, migrants crossed from Asia into North America. Some traveled across a northern land bridge that once connected the two continents. The bridge was located between present-day Siberia and Alaska. It is also possible that some travelers came to North America using water routes across the Pacific Ocean. In time, these early peoples spread throughout North America, finally reaching the Minnesota region.

Early Minnesotans

Generation after generation of these people fished and hunted wild animals for food and clothing. They lived in villages and caves and learned to carve stone and bone and later to shape copper into tools. To honor their dead, some of these people—now known as Mound Builders—built huge mounds made of earth. A few mounds remain within the state to this day. Grand Mound near International Falls is 100 feet long and 45 feet high. It serves as one of the largest reminders of the Mound Builders' long-ago lives. Some of the mounds contain valuable treasures.

Two girls pull a baby in a homemade box sled in Beltrami County around 1910.

Early Native Americans made the canoes that they used while spearfishing in the rivers and lakes.

A 9,000-year-old spear was once found in a mound located in Mille Lacs Kathio State Park in central Minnesota.

Many believe that early Native Americans were the descendants of the Mound Builders. Before European settlement, several Native American groups lived in the region that is now Minnesota. The Cree hunted and fished in the northern forests. The Cheyenne farmed and hunted along the Mississippi River.

Much of the state, however, belonged to the Dakota. They fished, trapped muskrat and beaver, hunted animals such as deer, and planted corn in eastern Minnesota. They moved with the seasons in search of food. The Dakota traveled from the woodlands to the flatlands, bringing their goods and tipis along with them. For centuries, the Dakota dug thin layers of red rock called pipestone from quarries. They carved the rock into pipes and jewelry for Sacred Pipe ceremonies. The Dakota believed that "the Great Spirit in the form of a bird . . . told his . . . children that this red stone was . . . sacred." Native people walked hundreds of miles to pipestone quarries in southwestern Minnesota to search for the soft rock.

In 1937, these quarries became the Pipestone National Monument, where only Native Americans could dig for the rocks. Today, the Dakota in Granite Falls still conduct Sacred Pipe ceremonies in the traditional way.

The Ojibwe, who are also sometimes called the Chippewa, moved into Minnesota from the east during the 1700s. Like some of the other Native American groups in the area, the Ojibwe lived according to the seasons. They hunted game animals but also harvested foods such as beans, rice, squash, and corn. Their homes were often near the water, so they built sturdy canoes out of birch trees. The Ojibwe lived in wigwams. These dome-shaped structures were made of wood tied together and then covered with bark. Tipis were sometimes used when the Ojibwe went on hunting trips. As the Ojibwe settled onto Dakota lands, the Dakota moved to the west and south. The two nations fought for decades. In the end, the Ojibwe forced the Dakota from many of their settlements.

In this painting by George Catlin, Ojibwe braves perform a traditional dance.

Making Model Snowshoes

Snowshoes let people walk on top of snow, and kept them from sinking. When Europeans and Americans first came to Minnesota, they were impressed by the snowshoes the Native Americans wore. Native Americans made their snowshoes out of animal hide and wood. You can make your model snowshoes out of pipe cleaners.

What You Need

Strong scissors
Seven brown or tan pipe-cleaners, each 12 inches long
Two pieces of embroidery thread or very thin string, each 4 to 5 feet long

Cut one pipe cleaner in thirds. Cut one of the three pieces in half.

Lay two brown pipe cleaners side by side. Wrap one of the smallest pipe-cleaner pieces around the pair at one end. Repeat at the other end. This makes the frame. Spread out the frame so it is widest in the middle and is pointed at both ends. It will make a leaf shape. Attach each of the two middle-sized pipe-cleaner pieces across the frame, somewhere between the middle and each end of the snowshoe. Wrap the ends of the pipe-cleaner pieces around the frame. These form the cross pieces.

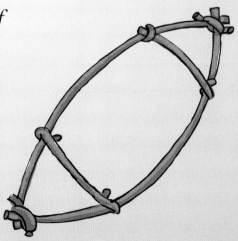

Tie the end of one piece of embroidery thread to a cross piece near the outside frame. Wrap it up and down around the two crosspieces over and over. When you have used nearly half of the thread, wrap it in the other direction, from side to side across the frame. Do not pull tight or you will change the shape of the frame. Tie the end of the thread to a cross piece or to the frame.

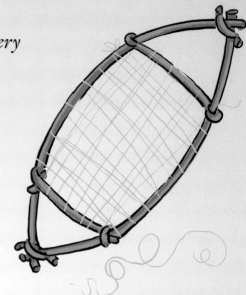

Bend one tip of the snowshoe up. This is the front.

Cut 1/4 of another pipe cleaner and loop it around several pieces of thread in the middle of the snowshoe. This would hold the person's foot onto the snowshoe.

Repeat the previous steps to create the other shoe. When you are finished, you can show them to your friends and family. You can also try to imagine what it must have been like for the Native Americans and early settlers who used these shoes while traveling through Minnesota's snowy wilderness.

French Explorers Arrive

The earliest Europeans to explore Minnesota were French fur traders. Several traveled through the Great Lakes region in search of a water route from the east to the Pacific Ocean. In the spring of 1660, Pierre Radisson and Médard Chouart, Sieur des Groseilliers, first explored parts of what is now southeastern Minnesota. They were looking for a route that would link the Atlantic and Pacific Oceans. They traveled through the state's many waterways, trading furs with the Native Americans along the way. Other traders, both French and English, saw the riches that Minnesota held and soon set off for the region.

In 1679, Daniel Greysolon, Sieur Du Luth, began his eleven-year journey through the area on behalf of France. He opened trade with the Dakota where the town of Duluth stands today. He also traveled with them to their villages in central Minnesota. Du Luth saw that the fur trade in the region could be profitable and claimed the region for the French king.

French forts were soon built along the upper Mississippi River and near Lake Superior. Most of the French traders who lived in the area respected the Native Americans' culture. The traders passed through Native American land without making trouble. A few French traders married native women. In exchange for the beaver pelts and other animal fur, the French gave the

French traders unload supplies at a port near their fort.

Native Americans European goods. These goods included woolen blankets, knives and pots made of iron, and guns. Little by little, the goods began to change the lives of Native Americans.

The biggest changes came after England won the French and Indian War in 1763. English traders with the Hudson Bay Company came to Minnesota. The English took over French fur trade routes. Eventually, most of the French moved from the area. But their influence on the region still remains today. Many rivers, roads, and towns, such as Elysian, Cloquet, and Belle Plaine, have French names.

Road to Statehood

In 1776, the American colonists declared themselves free from British rule. The Revolutionary War lasted for several years before the United States became an independent country. After the war, the new U.S. government wanted to expand westward. In 1803 it bought a large area of land from France. The region included present-day Minnesota. This agreement was called the Louisiana Purchase.

At first, English fur traders continued to work in the region. The U.S. government sent a small troop of soldiers to force English traders into Canada. Lieutenant Zebulon Pike found the perfect spot for a U.S. fort. The land where the Minnesota and Mississippi Rivers met belonged to the Dakota. In 1805, Pike traded whiskey and goods for the Dakota land.

The chiefs probably had no inkling [idea] that as a result of accepting Pike's glittering presents the U.S. Army would soon arrive to claim sovereignty [control] and build a fort on their territory.

—Historian Tom Severin.

This John Casper Wild painting shows Fort Snelling, the Mississippi River, and the surrounding settlements.

Fourteen years later, Colonel Josiah Snelling ordered that a fort be built near the Falls of Saint Anthony. This was the only waterfall along the Mississippi River. The settlement was first named Fort Saint Anthony but was later called Fort Snelling to honor the colonel's work. The fort became the first major settlement in the future state. It had Minnesota's earliest post office, school, and hospital.

Pioneers also built a flour mill and a lumber mill close to the falls to use the power of the tumbling water. The mills attracted immigrant workers, who settled nearby. Years later, the bustling settlement of Saint Anthony expanded into the city of Minneapolis.

More people came to the area, arriving by steamboat along the Minnesota and Mississippi Rivers. Military parties also arrived. They were sent to explore the land and to make sure that

Minnesota

it would be safe for American settlers. The settlers came, seeking farm land and trees for lumber. Missionaries arrived to bring religion to the pioneers and to the Native Americans. Parts of the state became more crowded and many people wished for more land. Only Native Americans stood in the way of land-hungry pioneers.

For the next thirty years, the U.S. government pressured the Dakota and Ojibwe for their valuable land. They agreed to many treaties that promised money, goods, and food in exchange for the land. Each treaty chipped away at more of the Native Americans' homeland and pushed them farther west.

The greatest changes in Native American territories in the area were a result of the treaties of 1851. These treaties required most Ojibwe to leave their forests in the upper half of the region. The Dakota sold all their land east of the Red River. In return, they received a small piece of land along the Minnesota River.

With the Native Americans relocated, settlers felt safer while traveling along the Mississippi River. Many steamboats docked at a landing downriver from the Falls of Saint Anthony. The landing, called Pig's Eye Landing, was named after a saloon keeper there. A missionary built the Saint Paul Church nearby.

Steamboats traveling northward on the Mississippi River brought people and goods to the growing region.

Pig's Eye Landing developed into a booming river port that grew into the city of Saint Paul.

Many settlers came to live on the open land. Villages sprang up along waterways and roads. Small farms owned by immigrants from England, Germany, and Ireland sprouted on the plains, making Minnesota a leading wheat producer. Settlers needed more building materials. This helped the region's logging industry. Saint Paul became the hub for boats. Six miles away, Saint Anthony expanded into a world leader for flour and lumber milling.

Between 1853 and 1857, the region's population grew from 40,000 to 150,000 people. The area was large enough to be considered a state. In 1858, Minnesota became the thirty-second state. Saint Paul was chosen as the capital.

Growing Pains

The new state continued to grow into the 1860s. The telegraph connected distant towns and established communication with the rest of the country. The U.S. government offered money to build a network of railroads. To find workers, railroad companies arranged to have steamship lines bring more immigrants into Minnesota.

At the same time, the U.S. government passed the 1862 Homestead Act. This law gave 160 acres of land to anyone who agreed to build and live on the land for five years. Many immigrants arrived from western and northern Europe, especially Sweden, Norway, and Germany. Some came seeking the freedom to practice their religion. Others left countries that demanded high taxes from their workers. The new settlers were happy to find land and a place where they could earn a good living.

By 1862, the Northern (Union) and Southern (Confederate) states fought over issues such as the right to own slaves. Minnesota belonged to the Union. It was the first state to offer soldiers. Governor Alexander Ramsey sent 1,000 Minnesotans to battle in the Civil War. Over the next three years, almost 21,000 Minnesota soldiers fought against Confederate troops.

Meanwhile, a different battle raged on Minnesota soil. This one was between the Dakota and the settlers. For years, the Dakota struggled with the terrible treatment they received from non-natives. The traders cheated them. The U.S. government rarely kept its promises. Each treaty reduced the size of their reservation. Native Americans were often given land without trees, so they had no place to hunt. They received rotten food and late payments for the land they had sold. With less land to hunt and farm, the Dakota grew hungrier and angrier.

On August 17, 1862, a small band of Dakota attacked settlers near Acton. Three white men and two women died. At first, Dakota chief Taoyateduta, or Little Crow, tried to keep peace. But other members of his band believed this was the best time to chase out the settlers because so many men were off fighting in the Civil War.

Dakota warriors attacked farms and forts. They burned buildings and killed about 500 settlers. Former governor Henry Sibley led a group of men that finally stopped the Dakota and captured 2,000 warriors. The following December, thirty-eight Dakota were executed in one of the government's largest mass killings. More were supposed to die, but President Abraham Lincoln pushed to have several released. Left with no other choice, the Dakota were forced onto reservations on the land that would later become South Dakota.

Farmers, Loggers, and Miners

The removal of the Dakota meant that even more land and resources were available to Minnesota settlers. The state was about to undergo another rapid growth in farming, logging, and mining.

Farms spread across the southern, central, and western regions. By 1878, wheat, Minnesota's main crop, filled about 70 percent of the state's fields. It was a major crop in the Red River Valley. This was good for the strong flour-milling industry in Minneapolis. Dairy products, corn, and soybeans also helped the economy.

In 1873, millions of grasshoppers swarmed across southwestern Minnesota, eating everything in their path. They returned regularly for the next four years to eat crops and even munch clothes that were hung out to dry.

These wood engravings display farm life in the Red River Valley in the late 1800s.

These men are breaking up a logjam that occurred on the Little Fork River.

The logging industry was originally centered just north of Minneapolis. Thousands of new immigrants earned their living by cutting trees and sending logs to the mills down the river. In the mills, workers cut the logs into boards. As loggers slowly cleared the forest, they moved farther north. The logging industry in Minnesota reached its peak at the beginning of the nineteenth century. Owners of lumber companies became rich. But they had cleared most of the state's white pines. By the early 1900s, one-third of Minnesota's trees were gone.

Logjams were common along the state's waterways. The worst was recorded in 1889. Logs backed up a 2-1/2 mile patch of the Saint Croix River, 100 feet deep.

In 1890, a miner working for the Merritt family discovered a large amount of iron in the Mesabi Range. Unlike other finds, this rich ore lay near the surface of the land. Workers could reach the valuable ore without digging deep mines. The first mine opened two years after the discovery. Soon tons of iron were shipped to eastern steel mills. Minnesota became a major iron producer.

In 1894, the Merritt family lost their mining company to wealthy easterners who owned larger companies. These bigger companies could afford to bring immigrants to dig in the mines. Work in the mines attracted many men from all over Europe, especially from Finland. Minnesota mining soon became a multi-million-dollar business. Taxes collected from iron mines paid for new Minnesota schools and other services.

Mining continued to be a major Minnesota industry into the twentieth century. In 1916, U.S. Steel—one of the largest steel companies at the time—opened a large plant near Duluth. The state was supplying almost three-fourths of the nation's iron ore. Within a few years, however, other countries found ways to ship iron more cheaply, and mining in the state started to decline.

Workers Speak Out

Large companies took over other industries such as manufacturing and food processing. They made owners rich but often left workers struggling to provide for themselves and their families. Minnesotans wanted their fair share.

The first major call for change came from farmers. Minnesota farmers paid high rates to store their crops in giant towers called grain elevators. They paid again to ship animals and crops to market. Since big companies owned most of the railroads, elevators, and milling companies, they could charge whatever they pleased. Farmers had no choice but to pay those high prices.

In 1867, a former Minnesota farmer named Oliver Hudson Kelley began a group called the National Grange. Members of this group wanted a strong organization that could fight for the rights of the farmers. The Grange spread rapidly throughout Minnesota. Members worked to reduce high shipping fees. They bought equipment and supplies as a group in order to lower costs. They also elected people who would pass laws to help farmers. During the early 1870s, the Grange pressured Minnesota lawmakers to enact the state's first law to control the

Children were expected to lend a hand on the family farm.

railroads. Officials listened, and a series of new laws to help farmers called the Grange Acts soon followed.

Minnesota is often called the Gopher State. The nickname came from an 1857 cartoon that represented railroad bosses as striped gophers. Gophers destroyed crops, just as railroads destroyed the earnings of farmers.

The National Grange was one of the first groups in the country that was open to both women and men. At a time when women could not vote or own property, the Grange's "Declaration of Purposes" read: "We proclaim it among our purposes to . . . (value) the abilities of woman . . . by admitting her to membership and position in our Order."

Through the years, iron workers banded together to push for better conditions, too. Some tried to strike and stopped working until owners met their demands. Similar walkouts occurred among northern Minnesota loggers, sawmill workers, and, later, truckers. Companies often responded by hiring men to break up the groups and force leaders to end the strike.

Minnesota's most famous strike came when Minneapolis truckers walked off the job. On July 20, 1934, police fired into a truckload of unarmed strikers. Several strikers died, and many more lay wounded. This would later be known as Bloody Friday.

Hard Times

Life was hard for most workers throughout the country from 1929 through the 1930s. This difficult time was called the

In 1935 these farmers brought their starving animals to the state capital. They wanted to show the lawmakers how the hard times were affecting Minnesota's farms.

Great Depression. Many businesses closed. One out of three Minnesota factory workers lost his or her job. More than half of the miners faced similar conditions.

Farming also hit hard times. Grain prices fell very low, and farmers could not afford to plant new crops. But Minnesota farmers continued to fight for their way of life. In 1932, farmers called a strike to get higher prices for their crops. They blocked roads to prevent food from being delivered to big-city markets. A year later, they marched to the state capitol in Saint Paul. This time, they helped pass a law to block banks from taking farms from families who owed money.

World War II helped end the Depression in Minnesota. Farmers produced food for soldiers, and iron was needed for war supplies. But after the war, the number of family farms started to decline. Many farm families moved into larger cities. In their place, large companies farmed corn, soybeans, and sugar beets. These crops were sent to processing plants in Minneapolis and Saint Paul. The companies also raised cows in the area that stretches from southeastern to central Minnesota, called the dairy belt.

Minnapolis and Saint Paul are known as the Twin Cities.

This successful dairy company in Robbinsdale had many trucks for delivering dairy products to its customers.

Loggers continued to chop red pine for lumber and cut black spruce, balsam fir, and aspen for the paper mills. Businesses and factories in the cities opened, making a variety of products from these raw materials. The Twin Cities expanded to include food, technical, and medical supply companies.

The mining industry started to decrease. Many U.S. Steel mills closed, forcing the residents of the Iron Range to seek other sources of income. Much of the region was turned into a recreation area.

Modern Minnesota

Minnesotans have always had a strong tradition of speaking out for themselves. This began with the National Grange. Rather than go along with the rest of the country, they created their own political groups. These groups addressed the specific needs of Minnesotans. One group was the Democratic-Farmer-Labor Party (DFL). National government figures of the 1960s and 1970s, Hubert Humphrey, Eugene McCarthy, and Walter Mondale, were three of the most well-known DFL members.

In 1998, state voters elected former wrestler and Minnesota native, Jesse Ventura as governor. Many Minnesotans wanted change in their state government and thought that Ventura could provide it. Ventura's term as governor lasted until 2003.

The state's long history of free thinking lives on. Recent battles have focused on schools, crime, the poor, and the environment. Minnesota continues to attract new residents who want to live in a place where people come first. As author Garrison Keillor wrote, Minnesota "produces good-hearted people who are tolerant, helpful and friendly."

Important Dates

1660   French traders Pierre Radisson and Médard Chouart, Sieur des Groseilliers, explore southeastern Minnesota.

1679   Daniel Greysolon, Sieur Du Luth, claims northeastern Minnesota for France.

Pierre Radisson

1803   The United States buys from France the area of America that includes Minnesota.

1805   Zebulon Pike buys Dakota land where the Minnesota and Mississippi Rivers meet.

1819   Colonel Josiah Snelling builds the first U.S. fort in Minnesota near the Falls of Saint Anthony.

1851   Most Dakota and Ojibwe forced from their Minnesota land.

1858   Minnesota becomes the thirty-second state.

1862   The Dakota Conflict rages between settlers and Indians, resulting in many deaths. Most Dakota are moved out of the state.

1867   Oliver Kelley begins the national farmers' group, the National Grange.

1873   Grasshoppers destroy crops across southwestern Minnesota.

1890   Iron ore is discovered in the Mesabi Range.

1890s   The logging industry in Minnesota reaches its peak.

1930-1935   More than half the iron ore taken from the earth comes from Minnesota mines.

1959   The Saint Lawrence Seaway opens, connecting the port at Duluth with the Atlantic Ocean.

Rosalie Wahl

1979   Rosalie Wahl becomes the first female state supreme court justice.

1991   Minnesota Twins win their second World Series.

1993   Terrible storms cause severe flooding along the Mississippi River, covering half the state.

1996   The Mall of America opens in suburban Minneapolis.

2002   Protesters camp outdoors in -30 degree weather for thirty days to stop loggers from cutting the last old white pine trees in Superior National Forest.

3 The People

Through the years, the hunt for jobs and land has brought waves of people to Minnesota. They arrived mostly from different states but also from other countries. Today, the state continues to attract newcomers. Minnesota is one of the fastest-growing states in the Midwest. People still come for jobs, but now they also look for good schools, lively mid-sized cities, quiet nature areas, and welcoming neighbors. These new faces arrive from a greater variety of places. Each group brings its own ideas, language, traditions, and holidays.

When the U.S. government last counted its citizens in 2000, Minnesota reported 4,919,479 people. This makes Minnesota the twenty-first most populated state in the nation. As with other midwestern states, Minnesota's population has shifted from country to city living. Almost three-fourths of Minnesotans now live in the larger cities of the southeast. The western and southern farm regions are left with fewer people.

However, many Minnesotans still think of themselves as country folk. As Greg Breining wrote, "I believe we think of

These Minnesotans are taking advantage of the snowy hills in Saint Paul.

43

ourselves as rural because we grew up 'on the farm,' or have parents who did. We enjoy getting out in the country and imagining we are part of nature again."

More than half of the state's population lives in the Minneapolis-Saint Paul region. Minneapolis has Minnesota's largest population with 382,618 people. Its twin city and the state capital, Saint Paul, comes in second with 287,151 residents. Minnesota's next largest cities are Duluth (86,918), Rochester (85,806), and Bloomington (85,172).

Besides having the largest population in the state, Minneapolis is also home to several thriving businesses.

Minnesota

Ethnic Diversity

The face of Minnesota has changed over the years. The earliest residents were Native Americans. Early settlers were mostly French-Canadian, Swedish, Norwegian, Danish, and Irish. Germans became the largest group, settling mostly in southern and central Minnesota. The late 1800s saw waves of immigrants from Poland and Czechoslovakia. People from Finland were the next to arrive. They settled mainly in the northeast.

A young girl of Swiss heritage participates in a cultural festival.

At first, these different groups kept their own languages and customs. Entire towns, such as New Ulm and Sleepy Eye, spoke German for decades. Years later, however, the daily life, traditions, and languages of these ethnic communities blended with the midwestern lifestyle. Today, Minnesota remains more than 89 percent European American. This number includes mostly people who were born in the state. As with the rest of the country, that trend is changing.

Starting in the 1970s, new immigrants began arriving from Southeast Asia and Africa. Large groups of people from Laos and Vietnam came after the Vietnam War. Vietnam was a dangerous place for many of the Vietnamese who sided with the United States during the war. A few Minnesota churches helped bring some of these Vietnamese to the United States. Between the 1970s and 1990s, Minnesotans helped about 40,000 Hmong Vietnamese immigrants who came to the state.

At first, many had difficulty adjusting to America and to life in Minnesota. But many Minnesotans went out of their way to make the newcomers welcome. Schools and medical centers hired workers who understood the immigrants' languages. The University of Minnesota created programs about their languages and cultures. Jim Eckert, a university historian, says, "Today, the state has the second largest population of Hmong and Tibetan in America."

Other ethnic groups have made Minnesota their home. During the 1920s, many Mexicans went from farm to farm picking crops with the seasons. Years later, many settled in Minnesota. Other Spanish-speaking people have joined them from the Carribean and Central and South America.

The Twin Cities have the greatest mix of residents. Hundreds of ethnic restaurants and stores that sell foreign products bring an international flavor to Minneapolis and Saint Paul. Some groups of immigrants tend to live in the same area. Hispanics have settled on the east side of Saint Paul.

Through the years many Mexican and Mexican-American families have made Minnesota their home.

Southeast Asians center around Nicollet Avenue South in Minneapolis and around University Avenue East in Saint Paul. Wherever immigrants settle, schools try to adjust to students who speak different languages.

Not all minorities are from other countries. About 3 percent of Minnesotans are African American. Some came to Minnesota as early fur traders and soldiers. More arrived after the Civil War. Most stayed in urban centers, such as in the Twin Cities. Alan Page, the Vikings football star who played in four Super Bowls, has been a Minnesota Supreme Court judge since 1994. From 1992 to 1996, Minneapolis lawyer Sharon Sayles Belton served as the city's mayor. She was the first African-American female mayor of a major U.S. city.

Minnesota's population is a mix of people from many different cultures.

Schoolchildren in Minneapolis learn about Native American artifacts and traditions.

Native Americans

Today more than 4 million Native Americans call Minnesota home. About one-third live in Minneapolis or Saint Paul. The Minneapolis Regional Native American Center was the country's first community center for Indians.

For years, native communities lacked money and the means to carry on their traditions. Now many of the eleven Indian nations in Minnesota invest in casinos, hotels, and related businesses. With increased income from these projects, more Native American Minnesotans are returning to reservations. There, they work to revive native traditions among their

people. At two Minnesota Historical Society museums in Mille Lacs and in Morton, non-Indians can learn about the first people to live in their state. "We have rooms that explain what Ojibwe did before Europeans," said Mille Lacs Museum guide Candace Sam. "And we have exhibits of modern housing developments, costumes for powwows, and recordings of Mille Lacs schoolchildren singing in Ojibwe."

These Ojibwe dancers are performing at a powwow at the Leech Lake Reservation.

Famous Minnesotans

Sinclair Lewis: Writer

The novelist Sinclair Lewis was born in 1885 in Sauk Centre. He turned his early life as a quiet, unpopular boy in a small Minnesota town into stories about everyday American life. He often wrote about women, race, and the plight of powerless people. In 1930, he became the first American to win the Nobel Prize in literature.

Briana Scurry: Athlete

Briana Scurry has been the USA Women's National Soccer Team's highest-ranking goalkeeper since 1994. She was born in Minneapolis in 1971 and lived in Dayton. She led the national team to World Cup and Olympic victories. She is now a top blocker for the Atlanta Beat soccer team.

Charles Schulz: Cartoonist

Everyone knows Charlie Brown, Lucy, and Snoopy. These cartoon characters were drawn by Minneapolis-born artist Charles Schulz. Schulz drew a weekly cartoon for a Saint Paul newspaper before creating the famous comic strip Peanuts. *Today,* Peanuts *characters are known and loved around the world.*

Patty Berg: Athlete

Patty Berg was born in Minneapolis in 1918 and is considered one of the best female golfers. She won more than eighty tournaments and was a founder of the Ladies Professional Golf Association (LPGA). In 1951, she was elected to the LPGA Tour Hall of Fame.

Gary Paulsen: Writer

Born in 1939, Gary Paulsen ran away from his Minneapolis home to join a carnival at the age of fourteen. He kept running until he had learned to act, sail, farm, or to do whatever crossed his path. He turned his adventures into action-packed stories for readers of all ages. Paulsen is a favorite children's author of more than forty books and hundreds of articles and short stories.

Bob Dylan: Singer, Songwriter

Songwriter Bob Dylan was born Robert Zimmerman in Duluth, in 1941. During the 1960s and 1970s, his folk and rock music called for peace and equal rights. In 1988 he was inducted into the Rock and Roll Hall of Fame. Dylan has received many awards and honors for his work.

Education is an important issue for many Minnesotans.

Schools for Everyone

Good schools draw families to Minnesota. Minnesotans pride themselves on a school system that includes everyone. When the first public school opened in 1849, Minnesota was the only state to educate girls and boys together. Today, Minnesotans continue to invest heavily in their children. The state spends more than most states on each student. Minnesota provides students with more computers than other states and allows students to enroll in better schools outside of their districts.

To encourage more schooling, Minnesota also offers free entry into state colleges. Because of these benefits, Minnesota enjoys the fourth-highest college graduation rate in the nation.

With a diverse population and bright hopes for the future, Minnesotans of all ages work together to make their state the best it can be.

These young Minnesotans know how important it is to give back to their communities. Here, students take part in a neighborhood clean-up.

Calendar of Events

Icebox Days

Every January the people of International Falls celebrate the winter season. Residents and visitors keep warm with a weekend filled with a candlelight ski, old-fashioned bonfire, ice skating, snowshoe races, snow and ice sculptures, and the "freeze yer gizzard" blizzard run.

Burns Night

On a chilly January night in 1857, Scottish farmers in Mapleton read Robert Burns's poetry to remember their homeland. Each January, the town continues the tradition with a poetry reading, Scottish songs and food, and bagpipe music.

Saint Paul Winter Carnival

In January, this city hosts the country's oldest and largest winter festival. Highlights include cultural celebrations, parades, contests, snow sculpting, exhibits, and an ice palace.

Lefse Dagen (Pancake Day)

In 1983, people from the town of Starbuck built a 10-foot by 10-foot griddle. The local baker prepared dough made from 30 pounds of potatoes, 35 pounds of flour, 1 pound of sugar, and 4 pounds of oil. Then everyone grilled and ate the largest pancake on record. Each May the town celebrates this event.

Festival of Nations

Since 1932, Saint Paul has hosted one of the nation's largest and oldest cultural celebrations. The event, which is held in late spring, includes days of dance, food, and art from various countries.

A Swedish festival

Finnish Fest

On the second Saturday in June, Embarrass honors its Finnish heritage with foods, crafts, and *pesapallo,* Finnish baseball games.

Land of the Loon Festival

In June, hundreds of Minnesotans gather in the city of Virginia to honor the state bird. Activities include a parade, arts and crafts displays, and foods from around the world.

Heritagefest

The entire town of New Ulm comes alive with an old-world German party in July. At the festival, tubas toot, singers trill, and crowds enjoy German foods, crafts, and costumes.

Lumberjack Days

In honor of the state's lumber history, Stillwater holds a parade, treasure hunt, and contests for log rolling, chainsaw carving, axe throwing, and speed pole climbing.

White Oak Rendezvous

Rendezvous is French for "great gathering." Each summer, visitors dressed as French fur traders camp at White Oak Fur Post, where they share meals and join in shooting, dancing, and singing.

Wacipi

Wacipi, which means "dance" in Dakota, is an important part of the powwows held each year in Mankato. The event remembers the thirty-eight Dakota who died after the Dakota Conflict and invites non-Dakota visitors to learn about the group's heritage.

Minnesota State Fair

The Twin Cities are home to a state fair that honors Minnesota's farmers. Agriculture exhibits, animal shows, and baking contests share the stage with musical acts and industrial displays.

A state fair

4 How It Works

Many government workers serve their state by helping to run the cities, counties, and townships. Minnesota has about 850 cities. About one hundred of these cities conduct business under home-rule charters. The state constitution gives them this right. It means that they may select the type of local government that fits their needs and then write their own set of rules, or charter. Many cities follow a form of government that includes a mayor and city council. The rest are run by commissioners or a council and city manager.

The state is divided into eighty-seven counties. A five-member board of commissioners manages each county. Board members decide money matters, such as how much to spend, borrow, and tax. Voters elect board members to four-year terms. They also elect a county attorney, medical examiner, sheriff, treasurer, and auditor for four-year terms.

Counties are also divided into townships made up of several cities and towns. Minnesota has about 1,800 townships. Each township has a board of supervisors that is elected for three-year

This statuary group, called "Progress of the State," is displayed on the capitol building in Saint Paul. The different parts represent civilization, prosperity, and the power of nature.

terms. The boards make sure daily life runs smoothly in Minnesota's many communities.

Statewide Government

Running Minnesota is a big job. Minnesotans elect lawmakers called legislators who serve in the state's two legislative bodies: the senate or the house of representatives. The senate includes sixty-seven members who each represent the district in which they live. The house of representatives contains 134 members. While senators serve four-year terms, representatives are elected for two-year terms. The legislature's main jobs are to create laws and decide how the state's money should be spent.

When you hold these positions, you learn that you're not just a spokesman for yourself. What I had to learn is that I also represent the state of Minnesota now.
—Former Governor Jesse Ventura

Minnesotans elect the governor, the state's chief officer, to a four-year term. In Minnesota, governors can return to office as many times as voters wish to re-elect them. The governor's job is to see that the citizens obey the law, to plan the state budget, and to appoint the heads of state departments, boards, and commissions. These officials help the governor carry out the state's programs and rules.

Fireworks explode over the State Capitol in Saint Paul.

How Bills Become Law

A bill is an idea for a new law or an idea to change an old law. Anyone can suggest an idea for a bill. But only someone from the legislative branch of government can move a bill through the steps required for it to become law.

Either a senator or representative must write the bill. A senator presents the bill in the senate, or a representative introduces it to the house. From there, the chief officer of that lawmaking body sends the bill to a committee.

Branches of Government

Executive The executive branch of government includes the governor, lieutenant governor, secretary of state, auditor, treasurer, and attorney general. Their chief jobs are to prepare state budgets and to make sure laws are carried out.

Legislative This branch consists of two houses: the senate and the house of representatives. The legislature's main job is to create and pass laws for the state.

Judicial Minnesota's court system rules on whether or not people have broken the law. The state Supreme Court heads the judicial branch. It has one chief justice and six associate judges. Under this court are the courts of appeals. These courts review decisions when people do not agree with the results from lower or district courts. Ten judicial districts are each represented by the district courts. District courts decide more serious cases in which two people or companies disagree.

This committee's job is to closely examine the bill. After much discussion, committee members advise the entire house or senate to either approve or reject the bill.

If the committee chooses to approve the bill, members of the legislative branch in which it began study its various parts as a group. Sometimes, legislators add or remove parts of the bill until they all agree. Once the bill passes in the branch in which it was first proposed, it moves to the other group of legislators for a vote. If the house or senate requests more changes, the bill then goes to a special committee in which representatives of both the house of representatives and the senate work out their differences.

After both houses pass the bill, it goes to the governor. The governor can sign the bill so it becomes law, veto or refuse to sign it, or let the bill become a law by not signing it. If the governor chooses to veto it, lawmakers can still make the bill into law with a two-thirds vote in the house and senate.

Helping Government Help You

"Our government was founded on the idea that anyone can make a difference," writes a Minnesota government official. "If you think those issues won't be of interest until you're older, think again." Minnesotans must be eighteen years old to vote. But that does not mean that younger people cannot have a say in what happens in their state. Young Minnesotans find many ways to participate in the state's government.

Project Citizen offers programs for students in grades six to nine. This program encourages students to work together to define a public problem, think of ways to solve it, and then develop a plan to put their ideas to work.

This young Minnesotan expresses his concern for state health care. Residents of all ages can become involved in state issues.

After writing the plan, students send their report to be judged by legislators and community leaders.

Minnesota students also let lawmakers know how they feel about issues affecting their state in a number of ways. They join groups that support issues that interest them. Or they share information by creating and passing out leaflets. Some students even plan speeches to present to government boards or committees. Many others write letters to local lawmakers and to newspapers.

Minnesota's young residents have affected many areas of government. In 1988, third-graders from Carlton decided Minnesota needed a state muffin like other states. They proposed the blueberry muffin because so many wild blueberries grow in northern Minnesota. Other ingredients used to make the muffins also come from farms across the state. To get their idea adopted, they searched for a legislator who agreed with them. He wrote and presented a bill that was signed by the governor. Thanks to Carlton's third graders, Minnesota now has an official state muffin.

Some students share their views and suggestions with state legislators. You can find the e-mail address of state representatives at www.house.leg.state.mn.us. The state senators' e-mail addresses are posted at www.senate.leg.state.mn.us.

In 1995, a group of junior high students from Henderson who were on a field trip noticed that too many frogs were deformed. As they studied how this could happen, they discovered that a similar problem occurred in Granite Falls in 1993. The Henderson students' discovery made headlines. The public was warned about the pollution in the Minnesota River wetlands. A house committee invited the students to present

These students attend an education rally at the capital.

their findings. The students brought photographs of frogs missing eyes and legs. They told the officials about the frogs that were born deformed because of the polluted wetlands. The house and senate discussed several ways to stop the problem. In the end, the legislature promised $151,000 to study the problem. This promise was part of a bill that became law in 1996. The study begun by those students continues to this day. It only proves that Minnesota residents of all ages can take an active part in the issues that concern their state.

5 Making a Living

Minnesotans work hard at a wide variety of jobs. They work on farms and in offices and factories. Many of these jobs turn the state's natural resources and raw materials into goods that are then sold nationwide. Minnesota universities and businesses join together to create new products and to improve old ones. Some common household items, such as adhesive tape and powdered milk, were invented in Minnesota. But not all Minnesota jobs involve creating and selling goods. Many of the state's largest industries, such as insurance and medical care, involve people helping others.

Farming Minnesota

Minnesota remains a major farm state. Half of the state's farm income comes from crops. Corn, soybeans, and hay are among the state's top farm products. Minnesotans also grow large amounts of wheat, sugar beets, oats, and barley. Peas, potatoes, blueberries, and apples are also important crops. In addition, Minnesota is the nation's largest producer of wild rice, a crop that was harvested by the state's first farmers, Native Americans.

Dairy farming is an important part of the state's economy.

Recipe for Wild Rice Soup

The Ojibwe and other native groups have been growing wild rice in Minnesota for hundreds of years. Minnesotans still produce this crop today. This delicious soup is a great start to any dinner.

Ingredients:

1 box seasoned wild rice
4 tablespoons butter
2 tablespoons minced onion
1 cup celery, chopped fine
1/2 cup flour
6 cups chicken broth
1-1/2 cup cream
1 teaspoon dried parsley
minced chives

Prepare the rice according to the instructions on the package. You can prepare the other ingredients while the rice is cooking.

Ask an adult to help you cut the onions and celery. Melt the butter and add the diced onion and celery. Have an adult help you cook this mixture until the pieces are soft. Add the flour and cook for two minutes, stirring often.

Next add the chicken broth, pepper, and parsley. Stir the mixture constantly until it becomes thicker. Add the cooked rice. Blend in the cream. Heat the soup but be careful not to bring it to a boil. Spoon into bowls and sprinkle some chives on top. When it is cool enough to eat, dig in and enjoy!

A young boy helps with the feeding at his family's hog farm.

Livestock provides the other half of the state's farm income. Southern Minnesotans raise hogs, beef cattle, and turkeys. The state's dairy cows bring in the most money. Most of the milk goes for making butter and cheese. The wealth of dairy products and grains produced in the state has earned Minnesota the nickname, the Bread and Butter State.

Unlike many states, some Minnesotans join cooperatives. These organizations help the farmers sell products and share the high cost of farming. The idea of cooperatives can be traced to the early Scandinavian immigrants. State laws in the early 1900s supported farmers who bought and sold goods as a group. Today, several thousand cooperatives work to store their products in creameries and grain elevators. This helps to lower their costs while increasing their profits.

Digging Minnesota

Mining continues to be one of Minnesota's biggest businesses. At one time, red iron ore accounted for most of the mining industry.

Besides making steel for the rest of the country, Minnesota's steel factories also provide jobs for thousands of state residents.

By the 1950s, though, most of the red ore had been mined. Miners then turned their attentions to a low-grade ore called taconite. They opened factories to make it into steel. Today, state factories send the steel around the world to be turned into automobiles, railways, tools, and utensils. Two-thirds of America's steel comes from Minnesota taconite mining.

Mining companies once built towns for the workers and their families near the open iron pits. As the mines grew larger, the towns moved farther away. In 1914, Swedish immigrant Carl Wickman started a bus service that brought miners from Hibbing to Alice. The company—now known as the Greyhound Bus Company—eventually grew and today provides transportation to thousands of stops around the country.

Minnesotans mine the earth for other materials as well. They remove gravel, sand, clay, and limestone from areas across the state. Companies also test Minnesota rock for large deposits of oil, titanium, and manganese.

Minnesota Manufacturing

Making crops into food products is a leading business in Minnesota. The state ranks fourth in the country for food processing. Minnesota is home to some of the world's biggest companies. General Mills, Pillsbury, and Land O' Lakes are just some of the companies based in Minnesota. They produce everything from cereals and snacks to butter and canned meats. Meat products such as Spam are Minnesota's largest food industry.

Trees are also still important to the state's industries. Making wood products is another key part of the state's economy. Aspens become paper and other wood products. Loggers chop oak and maple trees. These are turned into many products, including furniture and railroad ties. Minnesota farmers also grow evergreens, which are used for Christmas trees.

Paper-making factories gave rise to the state's second-largest industry, publishing. Because Minnesota sits in the center of the country, the cost of mailing products is cheaper. As a result, publishing has greatly expanded in the state over the past decade. About 55,000 people produce books, magazines, and other printed paper goods.

Minnesotans love Paul Bunyan—the legendary wood-cutting giant—and his pet ox Babe. According to one story, Bunyan cleared an entire forest with a single sweep of his ax. The Red River Lumber Company first created Paul for a 1914 ad booklet titled *Paul Bunyan and His Big Blue Ox*. Today, statues of Paul Bunyan stand in Bemidji and Akeley.

Technology is one of Minnesota's fastest-growing industries. Factories turn out everything from supercomputers and computer software to the latest medical supplies. Important health-care breakthroughs include blood pumps, pacemakers for damaged hearts, and hearing aids.

Products & Resources

Corn

Southern and southwestern Minnesota sit in the midwestern corn belt. This is where farms grow large amounts of corn. Some corn is shipped and sold to different parts of the country, but most is used to feed beef cattle nationwide.

Computers and Electronics

Minnesota manufactures more electronics than any other product. Computers, telephones, and medical instruments are made in factories across the state.

Flour

The state grows less wheat than in the past. But it still leads the nation in turning wheat into flour. Large companies make the flour into foods, such as cereals and cake mixes.

Dairy Farms

With more than 800,000 dairy cattle, Minnesota is a leading milk producer. Much of the milk becomes butter and cheese.

Pulp and Paper

Forests cover about one-third of the state. They provide timber for scrap board and paper products. Large paper mills can be found in International Falls, Grand Rapids, Sartell, Cloquet, and Brainerd.

Iron

Large iron deposits still lie in the Mesabi and Cuyuna Ranges. Once it is mined, the iron is sent by train to Lake Superior ports. It leaves the ports and travels by ship to steel mills.

Service and Tourism

The largest number of Minnesotans works in service industries. These are the telephone and transportation companies, banks, hotels, stores, and other companies that serve customers. Twelve thousand people work at the Mall of America. With more than 520 stores and an indoor amusement park, the mall is the largest in the world. Besides selling products, the mall is part of Minnesota's tourism industry. The mall attracts more than 40 million visitors every year. It draws more people than the Grand Canyon, Disney World, and Elvis's home, Graceland, combined.

The next biggest tourist attraction is the outdoors. Nearly one in two Minnesotans buys a fishing license, and one in six owns a boat. Many people from around the country travel to the state to enjoy its waters,

On a warm and sunny day visitors and residents fish along many of the state's peaceful waterways.

woods, and fields. "We have the longest state trail system and second most hunting acreage of any state," wrote outdoorsman Greg Breining. Fans of winter sports love to ride across the snowy land in snowmobiles. The first snowmobile was invented in Minnesota to help residents get around during the snowy winters.

Besides participating in Minnesota's outdoor and indoor sports, visitors and residents like to root for the state's professional sports teams. The Lynx are Minnesota's professional women's basketball team, while the Timberwolves are the men's professional team. Minnesota's representatives in Major League baseball are the Twins. The team was named after the Twin Cities. Fans cheer on the Minnesota Vikings during football season. Minnesota hockey fans root for their home team, the Wild.

Helping People

One of the highlights of Minnesota is its quality health care. At the turn of the century, Rochester doctors Will and Charlie Mayo and their father, William, discovered new ways to treat people who were ill. The Mayo family treated many patients and helped other doctors learn the latest methods and operations.

Their medical practice and hospital eventually expanded into the Mayo Clinics. Today, the Mayo Clinics include three large hospitals in Minnesota, Arizona, and Florida. They provide work for more than 2,300 doctors and 35,000 other workers. The Rochester clinic admits and treats many people each day. Because of its focus on good health care, Minnesota is ranked as the healthiest state in the nation.

The Right Balance

Mining, manufacturing, and tourism continue to attract new businesses. The problem, however, is finding a balance between creating jobs and keeping families and the environment safe.

Over the years, Minnesotans have battled over how to best use their land and water. Along the Minnesota River, farmers, home owners, and industries clash over water quality. The Boundary Waters Canoe Area Wilderness bans motorboats in order to reduce noise and motor-oil pollution. And those worried about threatened birds and animals work with logging and mining companies to find ways to save the forests where the creatures live.

Although its air pollution record is better than most states, Minnesota has issued about twelve alerts for bad air in the past thirty years. To clean the air, the state has passed laws to rid unhealthy areas of smoke, ash, and other pollutants. Minnesota reaches out to all its citizens, hoping to improve their lives. The state looks to a future when all Minnesotans can prosper in a healthier and safer environment.

These girls are on the lookout for Minnesota's native birds. By learning to appreciate their state's natural resources, residents of all ages are helping to make Minnesota's future brighter.

Minnesota's flag is royal blue with the state seal in the center. A wreath appears around the seal. The wreath displays the state flower along with three years: 1858 (the year of statehood), 1819 (the year Fort Snelling was established), and 1893 (the year the first flag was adopted). Because Minnesota was the nineteenth state, nineteen stars are on the flag.

The state seal shows a farmer on his field near the Mississippi River and a Native American on horseback. The state motto, "Star of the North," appears in French above the two men.

MINNESOTA

CANADA

Red Lake Reservation · Oak Island

Noyes · Pinecreek

Lake of the Woods

Roseau River · Lost River State Forest · Muskeg Bay

Thief Lake · 11

Red River of the North

11 · 59

Fort Francis · International Falls

Grand Mound · Voyageurs National Park

Red Lake Reservation · Kabetogama Lake

Mud Lake · Koochiching State Forest · 53

Grand Portage Reservation

Agassiz National Wildlife Refuge · Upper Red Lake

Bois Forte (Nett Lake) Reservation · Superior National Forest · Superior National Forest · Eagle Mountain · Grand Portage National Monument

Grand Forks · 75 · Thief River Falls

2 · Thief River

RedLake State Forest · 71 · Bois Forte (Deer Creek) Reservation

Vermillion Lake · Bois Forte

Grand Portage State Forest · Grand Portage

Red Lake Reservation · Lower Red Lake

Mississippi Headwaters State Forest

MESABI RANGE · 169 · VERMILLION RANGE · Superior National Forest · 61

White Earth Reservation · Paul Bunyan State Forest · Bemidji

Lake Winnibigoshish · Chisholm · Virginia · Lake Superior

Marsh River · Wild Rice River · Itasca State Park · Leech Lake Reservation · Leech Lake · Grand Rapids · 169 · Hibbing · 53

Moorhead · Buffalo River · Lake Itasca · Tamarac National Wildlife Refuge · Mississippi River · Savanna State Forest · Island Lake · Cloquet River · Split Rock Lighthouse State Park

10 · Detroit Lakes · 210 · Fond du Lac Reservation · Duluth

Fergus Falls · 94 · 52 · 71 · 371 · CUTUNA RANGE · 210

Brainerd · Kettle River · 35 · 61

Wahpeton · Mississippi River · Mille Lacs Lake · Snake River · Sand River

Alexandria · Little Falls · 371 · Mille Lacs Reservation · Rum River · SaintCroix National Scenic Riverway

Starbuck · 94 · 52 · 10 · Saint Cloud · 169 · Cambridge · Saint Croix River

Morris · Glacial Lakes State Park · Sauk River · Oak Grove

Big Stone National Wildlife Refuge · Chippewa River · Willmar · Saint Michael · Maple Grove · 694 · 61 · Saint Paul

Montevideo · 71 · Hutchinson · Minneapolis · 494 · 94 · 76 · Cottage Grove

Lac qui Parle River · Minnesota River · 212 · Belle Plaine · Shakopee Reservation · Prairie Island Community · Red Wing

Upper Sioux Reservation · Blue Earth River · Northfield · Red Wing · Richard J. Dorer Memorial Hardwood State Forest

Yellow Medicine River · Redwood Falls · New Ulm · 169 · 35 · North Fork River · 52 · 61

Marshall · Redwood River · Lower Sioux Indian Reservation · Swan Lake · Mankato · Zumbro River · Winona · Mississippi River

Cottonwood River · Pipestone National Monument · 59 · Des Moines River · Watonwan River · Blue Earth River · Minnesota Lake · 14 · Rochester · Cedar River · 90 · 63 · Root River · Richard J. Dorer Memorial Hardwood State Forest

Worthington · 90 · Fairmont · Albert Lea · Granger

Steen

Legend

Interstate Highway	Highest Point in the State	National Forest	National Monument	State Capital
U.S. Highway	State Forest	State Park	Indian Reservation	City or Town
State Highway	National Park	Wildlife Refuge	Boundary Waters Canoe Area Wilderness	

miles
0 · 20

76

Hail! Minnesota

Words by Truman Elwell Rickard and Arthur Wheelock Upson
Music by Truman Elwell Rickard

Min - ne - so - ta, Hail to thee! Hail to thee our state so dear. Thy ___ light shall ev - er be A ___ bea - con bright and clear. Thy ___ sons and daugh - ters true Will pro - claim thee near and far. They shall guard thy fame and a - dore thy name; Thou shalt be their North - ern Star.

State Song

More About Minnesota

Books

About the State

Butler, Dori Hillestad. *M Is for Minnesota*. Minneapolis: University of Minnesota Press, 1998.

Ciment, James., ed. *Scholastic Encyclopedia of the North American Indian*. New York: Scholastic, Inc., 1996.

Schwabacher, Martin. *Minnesota*. New York: Benchmark Books, 1999.

Of Special Interest

Helminski, Peg. *Kidding around Minneapolis/St. Paul*. Santa Fe, NM: John Muir Publications, 1996.

Lourie, Peter. *Mississippi River: A Journey down the Father of Waters*. Honesdale, PA: Boyds Mills Press, 2000

Paulsen, Gary. *The Foxman*. New York: Puffin, 1990.

Web Sites

Official State of Minnesota Homepage:

http://www.state.mn.us

Minnesota Department of Tourism:

http://www.exploreminnesota.com

Minnesota Department of Natural Resources:

http://www.dnr.state.mn.us

About the Author

Marlene Targ Brill writes about many topics, from history and biographies to sports, world peace, and tooth fairies. Each of her fifty books takes her on another journey, where she sees exciting places and meets interesting people. Minnesota is one of those places. Before writing, Marlene taught students with special needs and teachers how to teach them. She lives near Chicago with her husband, Richard, daughter, Alison, and their dog, Fluffy.

Index

Page numbers in **boldface** are illustrations.